2001 Jane Kenyon Chapbook Award

An Ordinary Day

An Ordinary Day

XUE DI

translated by *Keith Waldrop*
with
Wang Ping
Iona Crook
Hil Anderson
Janet Tan

Alice James Books
Farmington, Maine

10 9 8 7 6 5 4 3 2 1

Alice James Books are published by the Alice James Poetry
Cooperative, Inc., an affiliate of the University of Maine at Farmington.

Alice James Books
238 Main Street
Farmington, ME 04938
www.umf.maine.edu/~ajb

Library of Congress Cataloging-in-Publication Data
Xue, Di, 1957–
    [Poems. English. Selections]
    An ordinary day/Xue Di; translated by Keith Waldrop with Wang
    Ping ... [et al.].
        p. cm.
    ISBN 1-882295-34-X
    I. Waldrop, Keith. II. Title.
PL2921.7.E42A28 2002
895.1'52--dc21   2002000062

Acknowledgements

Some of these translations were first published in *Tyuonyi, Manoa, Hanging Loose, Arts & Letters, The Asian Pacific American Journal, The Temple, The Providence Journal, The World, Mid-American Review, Moonrabbit Review,* and *Cathay*; and the anthologies, *New Generation: Poems from China Today, This Same Sky, Poems from the Heron Clan, In Other Words,* and *The Constitution of Mercy*; and *Flames* (Paradigm Press); *Heart into Soil* (Burning Deck & Lost Roads).

In gratitude to Artemis A. Joukowsky for his generous support.

Cover image: Guo Jin, *Acrobatic Girls No. 2* (1999), oil on canvas. Courtesy of Chinese Contemporary Ltd., 21 Dering Street, London, W1R 9AA, UK.

Alice James Books gratefully acknowledges support from the University of Maine at Farmington and the National Endowment for the Arts.

for my sister xiao hong

Contents

An Ordinary Day

Injured Portrait

[van Gogh: "Self-Portrait with Bandaged Ear and Pipe," 1889]

When music deserts the human heart, when
squirrels leap into pine cones, when antelopes
frisk on the ocean floor
when leaf shrinks back to branch, refusing point blank
to fall
we will all be empty vessels, our
vague eyes anthills strung along
beams of light, insect egg-sacs
cemented to the heart, mouths
reduced to maledictions against barnyard animals
Everything, everything enrages me: this
nation of wild beasts, falling into decline
And as for poetry: a
stick between the jaws to block my bite

My ear: a sky-blue gem
touched by the crying of bugs
—summer lives inside. Place for a badger
to warm his paws night long. O deep
blue flame. Blue gem. My grandmother's
hands gripping the cow's udders
my irritable father: behold
a village, stately, its lonely glow
lighting my forlorn heart

Swarm of locusts! your chomp
encompasses earth. The people
are deaf and dumb, their ears no better than
saucers tied together by a string through the skull

Crocodile! Crocodile! my loved one, blue
blue gem, my aching
aching heart. Lop it off! Light
Light barricades my head. The sun
suddenly drops, warming the creatures
prancing in my blood
O gem, kingfisher-blue, to whom
shall I give you? who will
take you? Only the unstopped ear
Whose heart will hear the sacred harmonies

The Gleaner

[van Gogh: "Peasant Woman Stooping," 1885]

Pure ox horn. Then cows curved over wooden buckets
Gold husks buried in mud. The earth, nourishment
Men slaughtering no one for grain

Then the land was given. At harvest time
houses went up between fields of wheat
Babies in baskets crying like tumbling fruit

Then you, a simple peasant girl
Your basket, from which a hare drank
and eight baby rabbits singing in your eyes

Grain! The village where childhood lived
where birds flew glittering like gold
attaching themselves to the neat river's face

Peasant girl! Round arms of a crescent moon
and bent like a crescent. Show me
how your forebears turn to gold in the soil's gift

Your fingers gleam with brightness
Wheat like a shower of diamonds
Watching you move with pious step

Girl, this heart—my heart—how
can it keep from falling into despair
in the ray of sunlight, close and airless

Sower

[van Gogh: "Sower with Setting Sun," 1888]

When the soil wakes from its deep sleep
sun paints the field's edges, revealing
a mouse's footprint baked into its surface
Wild geese begin their game with summer
Take their eggs, place them
over the lizard's fragile burrow. Fields

bulge up. The horses have galloped off
Give the odor of their groin to the swaying
cradle of the moon. I sit
inside the daisy girl's long flute
and feel earth's burgeoning desires

And just at this moment, you come
striding out of the sun, long stride across the
lumpy earth. Joy's radiance
turns your whole body to the dark
Grains gnaw at you. The land bleeds
You hear fruits crack open in the sky

Thinker among cattle, human
tongue of steel, your body
pressed to the dirt. All winter
you clutch the seeds and when you
open your fist, I wake to spring
watching your golden wheatfields sprout in blood

What joy! A mental halo
glazes the growing field
Your coming is mankind's primal song
I follow a foal as it wanders the riverbank
grazing on fruit blown down in the dusk

Remembering

Words! before you led me to destruction
the guava seed was a clean hand
prodding me to get on my way
I've torn the skins of things, like crushing grapes
My heart spread its wings
hovered in the round heart of the wine
Men's faces, then, stood in oil
Had I ever used the word *detest*?

My mouth is a horse's mouth
—language my hay, dried in sun and air
The feet of birds are buried under the hay
lizards on one side building a nest
Talking about them causes me an
animal pain
Takes my hand, places it on the word
to find the spot from which feelers sprout

Childhood! My poems a clean house
the fields a ball rolling
Mother's two baskets on a pole across her shoulder
Over emerald leaves, rivers rush on
Had I ever worn the anxious look I wear now?
Make my poems a rag to wipe with—wash here, wash there
Make grating sounds—wrench here, wrench there
Throw the books on the floor
From a snowy sky remote from humanity
snowflakes striking become soundless tears
Had I ever tried to praise beauty?

My entire body glittering quicksilver
my first song was in my youth
My teeth shone then like the horns of a fawn
in the pride of life, my smile unhidden
I walked then
like water drawn from a well

Remembering! This conch shell
Golden yellow makes me see
the flesh that quivers within life
Sound of stones contracting
The sound of flesh
Waves washing over strands of sinew
The drowned become shells
and in my breathing speak their understanding
of a world that follows after death
Vengeance on the living, through silent sounds
Remember! Trees felled and dry and rotten
Ants on a stump
crawling in a ring
Light encircles you
People—in moving forward, they fall
into the deepest dark. The most
radical among them try hardest to look out
drawing nearer, day by day, unfeeling flesh
Seeking that conch
we are still children
laughing at the sky

Words! before you lead me to destruction
I want to see clearly your real shape
Living among people, I am
a wolf, not yet grown into exile
avoiding the traps of words, of phrases
All around me, throats steeped in venom
swaying in the barrens! The four seasons
hide within men's eyes
revealing the spots of the leopard
My heart, how can you not press your lips
to patches of sunlight in the mud?
How can you not wail for an animal?
An infant rises before me
flexes four limbs, cries
Earth glitters, not yet fouled by men
Then how can I not sing?
One after another my poems
make the sound of chains shaken
one of my legs crushed by the crowd
my cry of indignation and despair

Crack the world to its core, you'll find a poem
Standing in the presence of poetry
is all that can make my whole body tremble
Hearing insects make love
my blood gushes from poetry's heart
words tumbling over each other

clambering over light-beams in the wheat
Empty conch shell. Anxiety and respect
together forge a brain. Still in a woman's womb
love, gleaming gold from head to foot, rising
on this fluid, a hand takes hold of the ocean's horn
From the moment a melody called to me
life showed me the delicate bones of men
filled with a marrow of purest gold and
praised by poetry
Our ancestors appreciated in silence
the sharp shards of those bones
the trembling of these healthy beasts
at life's very center
Fields of flowers opened by light

My heart! Could you then pronounce
from your precious lips the filthy
word *detest*?

The Mushroom River

That river is filled with mushrooms
  Yes, mother. The river you soaked your hands in
  My past flows by. The child in his red jacket exposes the
  skin of daylight. He is picking mushrooms on the river, his
  basket full of smiles
  Do not enter the dark misery of the forest. Mother

come back to the fairy tales with me:
  grandma hides the wolf in your voice, baring the day's teeth
  It's getting dark again. Will my love get lost? Mother, my
  childhood is gone forever
  Your hands bring the sound of water brimming from my eyes
  Do not go the lonely path of old age. Mother

Mushrooms. Butterflies dance in your silver hair
  The light is on. I walk towards you, along the river. The
  wolf in the fairy tale will die too, and the child do riffs
  on its teeth to go with the beautiful sounds of the road
  Memory pushes up like no end of pale, floating mushrooms
  carrying off the last of your years
  Go back inside. Don't stand in pain, waiting for me
  Remember how my poems send signals. I'll bring you songs of
  the vast fields

I'll describe for you the mushroom river

The Town Drunk

Soft night presses down on me
I hear the sad horn of the setting sun
It wiped the day's bronze mouth and
entered memory's dark cave
There's a wise man
thrusts water from him
I recognize the smell

How can a wolf survive the city
scratches himself against the stairs
crowds himself into the crowd
leg stained with wild berries. His
nose frozen, like a man's feet sticking
out from under the blanket
The sun's head is scarlet. Glass
cuts through his limbs like water
In dead of night I hear the howl
of dreamers on the run

My face
is woven like a bamboo basket
Soft night nestles me gently
The dark along my throat enters
the heart. In the wine's bright light
    I hear
his murmur and my murmur back
feel his hand

etching its loneliness
in the silver liquid. From memory's lair
a golden trumpet sounds

A buxom woman
draws all happiness
into her bright breasts
In the holy valley, covered with milkweed
you drive red foxes
I douse my flesh
in the shadow of their eyes
A hand sweeps the river
into death's panorama
The light flashes and goes out, leaving
bloody stains behind. The heart of blood:
night stirs the brimming past

Hatred! A big garish bird
darts through my throat into the sky
 depositing in my
 life her rock-like eggs
Scorpions nest under stones
snakes bask in the momentary sun
spring and summer take turns
trying to break my bones
Autumn's in the distant song
in dreams. Bees
sting busy travelers' cheeks

Pain! Hatred! My
city built with hollow bricks
bears the imprint of burnt grass
    Glass reflects
    patterns of water
Humans live within
    filling the hollows
The buildings stand for sex organs
Look at that man: that
    beautiful hollow human
is machine–made
He holds the same grass
and has to ask about his own face
Teeth, white enamel
gnashes the language of the dead
That river looks like a day
squeezed between two
nights. Pain! Disgust!
At night, my
limbs, you
hear doomsday coming

Where, in the pure
liquid, is purity?
I still see empty darkness
like the ring my lover gave me at the wedding

My wine, holy music
   covers my rocky beach
   my small mole cricket
In the thick shiny moss
I still see
a face I can't get rid of
   Teeth glint
on the rim of my wine glass
The city nests in my hair, like a beast
listening to horror chew at me
the pure clear liquid entering my veins
Pain! Pain! Born with me. Singing
through the four seasons. Laughing
Ablaze
   Piercing the dark
   Loneliness

I grasp
pain in its reflection
Blood talks to life through cracked skin
Pure red flowers
   open into shells
They remind me of some gorgeous fish
motionless behind a rock
My heart sinks in the water
talking casually with the long dead
Oh no, you can't see! That darkness
changed my face. The sun's hand

pulls my hand under the night
lets me know that in every object
there's a perfect stone
lets me know my lover
is also grass. Under her feet
the insects, who live brief lives
chirp the four seasons through. Let my lips
touch glass-thin praise. Whenever you wake
you see something surprising. Press
close to it! with your brilliant pain

Interplay

The living
are shadows of the dead
They make noise
When the dead dream in the silent dark
when the dead wake
the living feel sudden terror
day-long loneliness
It is the dead
who have left home
to meet their family on the way
The living, day by day, age
It is the dead who try to
return to the world
The living feel alone
when they meet each other
They shout "Who
loves me?"
It is the dead standing
next to them
The dead clench their teeth
with contempt
with revenge
Because the living
are always giving the dead a bad name

Zone

There's water there, the garden opens
Singing, you wear your red skirt
Summer is a pattern of
flowers on your sash
Days pass
as you turn. Birds
fold their wings ten thousand ways
All this time I'm far from home
Along the road, wheat fields breathe from
their broad lungs, the land
sends out clear noises. All this
time, I'm trying to get across it
Soil circles earth
I've a thousand expressions
to display my yellow face
Wheat fields hum a song
   —in the East

There's steel. Highways
cut through what used to be fields
Jazz bleats
in the shadow of high buildings
There, the homeless
find wheat fields in their dreams
At the blast of ten trumpets a new
continent arises and the sea

rolls the passion of sex. In the East
the voice of home
breaks up each day. I cover my face
sobbing among ruins
Still I try to track
the zone I dream of. On my way
seeing my youth, seeing
middle age mounting me
like two sharp and
shiny rib bones
hampering my breath
here on western land
I find that any direction I
walk, every impulse whatever
points clearly, unambiguously
　　towards—China

Homing

As I walk homeward
dusk surrounding
in groups behind me wanderers
sing out their songs of labor
carrying their hands as they would carry money
carefree, never asking where they're headed
Since I left youth behind
I see my days each day in strangers. Once I
sang from waywardness
happy in my passion. Each day
a line of poetry. For all the things
I seek and for those I curse

As I step onto that road
that cuts empty and still through overgrowth
rivers glitter around me
The world I entered once and wasted
sways in my heart with a gentle sweetness
I touch the soil in quiet ecstasy
Things crowd around me
each singing in its bound
For the first time, I hold my head up
In that light I need no language
to express my gratitude
Youth has fully ripened, as fruit
bodies out between pit and skin
my poems press out around my heart
simple and full of feeling

holding the dreams and the labor
of a life of pain

As I walk this plain of consciousness
in a fullness of light
where every object vanishes
reappears, metamorphoses
I feel "home"
inside my body
and these pains and aspirations
though together in one
dwelling, belong to different centuries and
different lives. Home gleams in my
blood. My blood
flows round the house which is
made of light. My bounding heart
beats in cadence with
this house radiating its
pure white beams

White Rubber Mask

I hold up this face. It looks out of
two eyes, with a wide open mouth
Now it brings to mind the Hopi
diminished after thirteen centuries
In one of their innumerable mystic rites
all the Hopi opened wide their mouths
to shout—but no sound came
I'm waking from sleep
Why is it so dark
in that wide open mouth? In that
screaming silent mouth I see always
death chasing death. I see death
crushing underfoot the teeth of creatures
Death never makes a sound. Death
merely appears, like that open mouth
The shout must come from us. Crowds vanish

Will my perplexities be resolved? My
thoughts trip up my feet and
haul me into greater horrors
Am I in a dream or on New Mexican mesa
I see the white rubber mask
human cries transmuted to "energy"
Matter still exists. It opens its
round mouth wide. Generation after
generation does battle and sinks
slowly out of sight invoking gods and spirits

Death's mouth is forced open
to let such desires and such travail
burst out—tragic, indignant, injured
This is the pueblo where the Indians live
Rivers have dried up. Dust drifts from
here to there. In my sleep
I hold up this white rubber mask
Three black holes confront me
It laughs. The rubber is thick
a hard and springy substance
I know already, before waking
I will wake in terror

Faces

When you stop thinking and trembling
your face like a piece of
cowhide scorching curls inward. Time
like mice runs through the ceiling beam. You
hear its quick and cautious scurrying. Your face
grows older in the silence. Inside your
body, you feel something quick and cautious
running through
A feeling like cowhide
curling inward slowly as it burns
light suspended along with
the curvature of things
In the surrounding dark and my
body's peace, I watch human
faces curled outward by a hundred years
peel like the bark from tree trunks
dessicated and resin-parched. Human faces
twisted and lost, peel away from the spirit
Violence creates a quiet in existence, fear
curved layer by layer into the heart of silence
Something quick and
cautious runs through human memory
bearing traces of burning, the grief
of things gone

So you feel when you stop
thinking and trembling. Morning late
you lie on your bed. Sun crosses your pillow

inch by inch. The room grows brighter
You're hearing the cry of things
irrevocably twisted

Earth

Dry-eyed, we gaze down the road
at parents and children returning: scattered
bones abandoned on the wasteland of memory
Each and every night the dead come back
carrying bouquets, wearing laundry-marked shirts
recognizing the sleepers. They guard us
When they leave, they leave their bouquets
next to our pillows. We wake, see the sunlight
Maybe we hear birds. Awake, we've
first of all the palpable recollection
of having been somewhere, having felt some
cold, having done something. Wide
awake: to wake is to forget
What shines is only the morning sun
and its light is not from life

Our eyes dry, an earth remote from us
eats, drinks, sickens us
bewitches and crazes us. Still
deeply in love, we
left our lovers. Leaving our
childhood there, we left our roots
Only in sleep do we
rejoin our relations. Each night
returning, quietly to feel
the familiar faces, before
dawn, before we wake

Since then, living between two realities
we age at double speed
sunk in a confusion of
everyday and inner worlds
We live and move along widening fissures
of fatigue, despair, dream, forgetfulness

Childhood remains on that earth
of no return. Sleeping
we make love to old lovers
loving again in sleep, kissing and
drinking that earth in on our lover's body
weeping for past love, writing for
love past, waking, wanting
to sleep again. Sitting in the sun, I
watch myself age towards that distant earth
aching to lift the light and the fruit that
loom in the loneliness, lifting them high
in the old love, here among untold strangers

Autobiography

Against darkness the shiny pelt
slides down. Night
chews the bones of tiny creatures
I try to see into the
past that pain has pressed shut
The white woman
watches me in her happiness
She doesn't understand how
I am full of anger, how
an armed government
can modify the soul
within a body
Ah, but the only indestructible
is flesh. It can
bend serenely in the dark while
the humiliated soul flees screaming

To squat at the root
of animality. Their sex
flickers in my brain
Something I must have
felt this dark night. My two
little fingers twist and
pinch the lips spitting out
the word "motherland." Motherland

source of my destitute wandering
abroad, in
shame. Against darkness
the shiny pelt. I weep for
love of the white woman. Pure love
Sublime love. I hate
my hysterical past

Who can stop him? Facing the
way he came, hateful and contemptuous
he turns humiliated and keeps on
walking. The night maintains
my body temperature. He wakes
from his long anger. Who can force him
back to it, whether
abroad or in his motherland
When the soul returns
existence is ratified
Flesh is weak but
strong if you feel the soul
Light shines out like matter
lifting you in clarity
You stand in the road and weep
weeping the fullness of love
and the only thing that can stop
you, finally

stop you, is
there are limits to
what a body can do

Nocturne on a New Theme

One after another, westward
we drive "love"—this
fashionable car. Its bumper
cuts through cheers and catcalls
Love cuts open our bodies. We
live in a strange country
Love between white and Asian
is a complicated
soup. N.B.: the white
drink soup as an appetizer
while to the Asian, soup means
end of banquet

To make love or to leave
whites like to shout at the
top of their lungs. The yellow
manage with a look. One after another
moving in the flesh. Only in bed
are humans allowed to air their
hate without reserve. Biting
cursing, backbiting—all
indicate succulent loving

Westward our love moves, on
four tires with a slow leak
Every night through the
pain of growth. Like a whacked nail

bent, we're making love. The love we've
made breaks through the gulf between
races—a work completed
in the dark. The flesh
shines. We know
who we are. Where
are we

The Passage to Heaven

I see him from a distance. Sleep
is a long narrow train with
many empty seats. I see myself
sitting, traveling somewhere
Along the way, on my left
I see unfold, meticulously, a
mysterious orange and ochre scape. I
almost wake up
Heaven is just back of my
eyes, almost as if—the train moving
just a bit faster or
stopping—I might become
the first person to see heaven
and return. I can't tell you
how that passage
woke me at midnight and made
me happy. The train reaches its
destination in the tropics. I'm
waking slowly and longing for
two women I love

Sweet Jazz

Love with care. Loving you
amber in sick flesh
east of China. When I love, a
pair of goat horns seems more
crooked. Our love's closest ocean's
salt flows into the
one dog's eye. Those labyrinthine
eyes once deeply loved

Those fires—the river at nightfall
carries them away. Horses vanish
night owl of the east. When torso and torso
like two lakes flow together, lips like
fish on a dive to the lake's bottom
Our love's closest village
all the ponies jolted from their dreams
   to happy waking

Internal Relations

Christened in whitest snow
A life-style the very image of
winter landscape. The horses, blue

crook their necks, sleep
soundly in the snow.
The child peels Chinese bananas

develops very thin life—
long, filled with spirit and good will
Darkness dances in his fine

symmetrical limbs. Riven, like
sex emerging naked in a core
of light. Together with a

pretty woman, kind-hearted, moist, the fire
surges up again. Yellow weasels gang up
screaming in a no-man's-land

Her face is radiant. Black night's
youngest psychic child
dissonant most when alone

Pheasants return in memory before sunset
Wild dogs traipse the snow in the
small town. The child called Xue

utterly lonely, fantasizes all day long
He has seen happiness, translucent, shining, shattered
heaviest snow of the year

New Year

Snow covers former days

Children hide in the snow while three squirrels
scurry to cross the road running between tree trunks

The trumpet blows the lips, extravagantly
wild with joy. Lover's anxiety
blessing like an abandoned factory

in this year's coldest rain. Cello
slithering, like a big bird on vacation
A feather, mother's best-loved child

in a foreign land, days grown old, even
lighter than a feather. Father, a pen

nearly fountained out, held
in the hand of his oldest farthest child
in exile, a soul alone

Spirit-filled child. Who feels most
the pain. Whose thought is deepest
And the flesh hardening

around his deep and anguished love. As in
a small harbor, fishing boats arrive on time
tourists gawk at seawater unloaded by the gallon

After which, mast and sails
point at a tilt. Birds, vacationing
done, fly north along the ocean axis

Snow presses down on shrunken
used-up days. Through the window
I see a new year, sunlight darkening

in a quiet little New England town
New Year—is my distant home

feeling the chill, a period of new blizzards

Circumstances

In the bikeshop basement, a repairman fits the
naked wheel. March, like a crazed sheep

Lovers leap longingly across Valentines
like black rain coming down in sunlight
Crowds collect, turning both directions

on cracked concrete roads. Tax money
maintains the smallest state stranded on the longest
polluted shore. Then come commercials

oozing with essence of female
pudenda. Private viruses made public
soothe the natives to stupor in sticky sheets

Fresh air aggravates craziness
We try to forget whatever we don't understand
powerless against distant antagonists. Reduced to

personal lives, we drift
dark and polluted streams
on the ground of freedom

An Ordinary Day

From darkness to darkness
halfway is even darker, a
path completely spiritual

Imagination makes day heavier
our flesh easier
among supposedly visible rays of light

so that wild animals, in the memory
of those earliest forgotten peoples, are
full of human nature. A tattooed child

eats meat in the shallow darkness
on his left ankle an anchor, resembling
the figure of a bird carrying a distant evil

flying away
The master of a new age arrives
his body full of holes and gilded rings

shining out of a darkness we know intimately
whose very end is the deepest darkness
spiritual darkness. Where

a body sits thinking, sad
solid, alone, like
a needle

Love in Difficulty

Reconciled
I feel close to the source
I am rocked in the long ark of
poetry. In another reality my hand
writes lines with the odor of plants
My body, in its difficult
times, enjoys them—keeping life
aware and
closer to the source. Pleasure without
self-consciousness. Life is a trembling
liquid, sending out strains of
unprompted praise
The ark of poetry
glides away and along
on this clear rippling
water
People love and feel loved, feel
happiness calm and pure

Love in difficulty is my
poem. One stanza is complete. In another
reality, a new stanza is being
born, but isn't yet there
I grope for lost arrivals
Life, through me, falls
weeping. Can't you feel the difficulty
of connecting the first line
with a whole life? The hardship of
this life makes life, in another

reality, glide
Much love turns us, vertiginous, takes
away suffering. The ark of poetry, at last
watertight, rises in the latest
days of this life. Water to
water. Water lifts water
in the clear calm of poetry
In my love's fullness I
bless those who still
have many lives to live

Forgetting

Six years of drought
Eye on the boats. River grows short

Man lost in a foreign land
speaking some other sort of language

closer to himself
The local scenery

smoke among rocks, dinnertime
through empty walls

Then the guests lift up their bodies
A river in a region without boats

tide rising. It's farther to my home town
speaking some other sort of language

asking for the road home. A flock of gray birds
carry drought from the mainland

Cold surging from crystals of
oblivion, strange things, transparent

Hotel Viking

In the wake of a prefabricated passenger ship
the ocean, as if with an old cotton blanket

weighs deeply on a body wide awake
The sky in the eyes of a scattered school of fish

grows brighter and brighter. The bridge that spans the
brine crosses also the opaque middle-aged mind

dark path between two precise terms
My mother grieving

writes to her faraway son
Waterbirds, lonely, follow the lights

toward regions of cold where they hover
This evening the hotel room's thermosystem

thundered without rest. Number 634
said the key in the unlit hallway

In my homeland some valuable
persons are disappearing

Translators

Injured Portrait	Iona Crook & Keith Waldrop
The Gleaner	Wang Ping & Keith Waldrop
Sower	Iona Crook & Keith Waldrop
Remembering	Iona Crook & Keith Waldrop
The Mushroom River	Wang Ping & Keith Waldrop
The Town Drunk	Wang Ping & Keith Waldrop
Interplay	Wang Ping & Keith Waldrop
Zone	Wang Ping & Keith Waldrop
Homing	Wang Ping & Keith Waldrop
White Rubber Mask	Wang Ping & Keith Waldrop
Faces	Janet Tan & Keith Waldrop
Earth	Wang Ping & Keith Waldrop
Autobiography	Wang Ping & Keith Waldrop
Nocturne on a New Theme	Wang Ping & Keith Waldrop
The Passage to Heaven	Wang Ping & Keith Waldrop
Sweet Jazz	Hil Anderson & Keith Waldrop
Internal Relations	Xue Di & Keith Waldrop
New Year	Xue Di & Keith Waldrop
Circumstances	Xue Di & Keith Waldrop
An Ordinary Day	Hil Anderson & Keith Waldrop
Love in Difficulty	Wang Ping & Keith Waldrop
Forgetting	Hil Anderson & Keith Waldrop
Hotel Viking	Hil Anderson & Keith Waldrop

Recent Titles from Alice James Books

Alice James Books has been publishing exclusively poetry since 1973. One of the few presses in the country that is run collectively, the cooperative selects manuscripts for publication through both regional and national annual competitions. New authors become active members of the cooperative, participating in the editorial decisions of the press. The press, which places an emphasis on publishing women poets, was named for Alice James, sister of William and Henry, whose gift for writing was ignored and whose fine journal did not appear in print until after her death.

PRINTING BY THOMSON-SHORE
DESIGN AND TYPESETTING BY LISA K. CLARK